99 WAYS TO DIE
IN THE MOVIES

First published 2016

Tumbleweed, and imprint of The History Press
The Mill, Brimscombe Port
Stroud, Gloucestershire, GL5 2QG
www.thehistorypress.co.uk

Concept created and images supplied by The Kobal Collection, 2016

British Library Cataloguing in Publication Data.
A catalogue record for this book is available from the
British Library.

ISBN 978 0 7509 7053 2

Design and origination by The History Press
Printed in Turkey by Imak.

99 WAYS TO DIE
IN THE MOVIES

DIAMONDS ARE FOREVER (1971)

DANJAQ/EON/UA/THE KOBAL COLLECTION

AMITYVILLE 3-D (1983)
DE LAURENTIIS/ORION/THE KOBAL COLLECTION

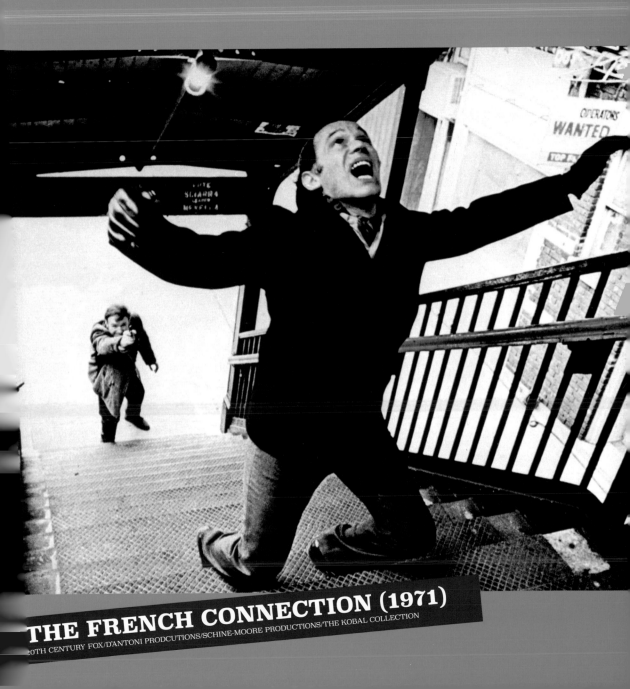

THE FRENCH CONNECTION (1971)

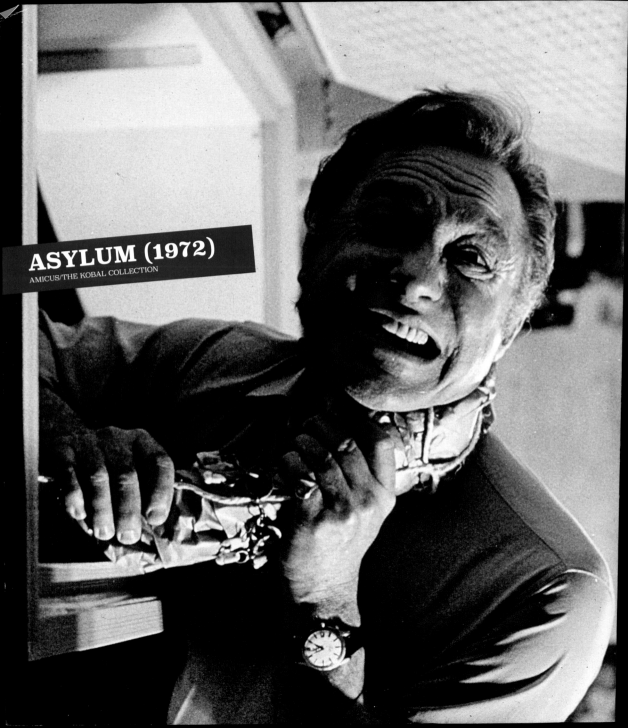

THE GODFATHER (1972)

PARAMOUNT PICTURES/THE KOBAL COLLECTION

ON THE WATERFRONT (1954)

BEETLEJUICE (1988)

GEFFEN/WARNER BROS/THE KOBAL COLLECTION

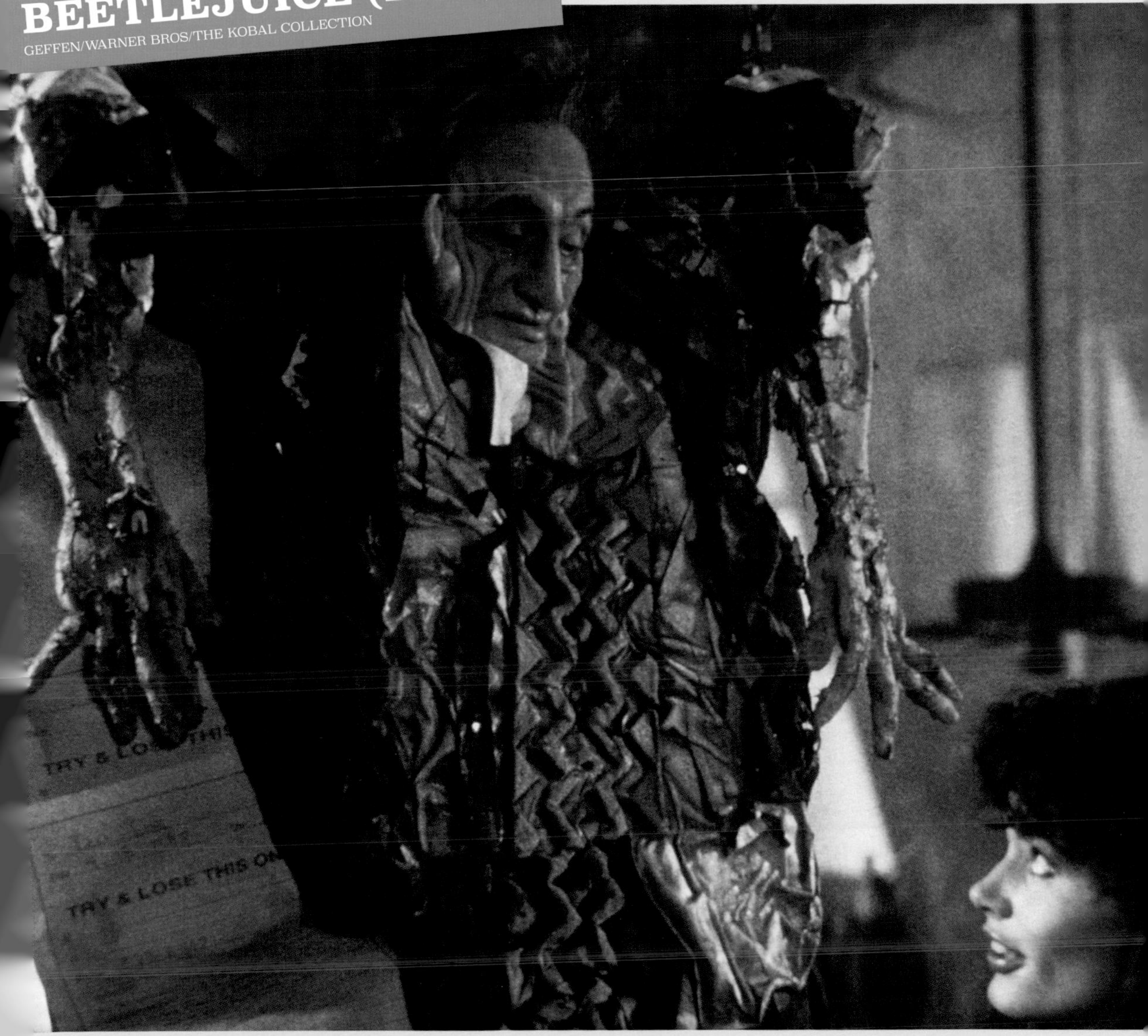

THE BLACK CAT (1966)

FALCON/HEMISPHERE/THE KOBAL COLLECTION

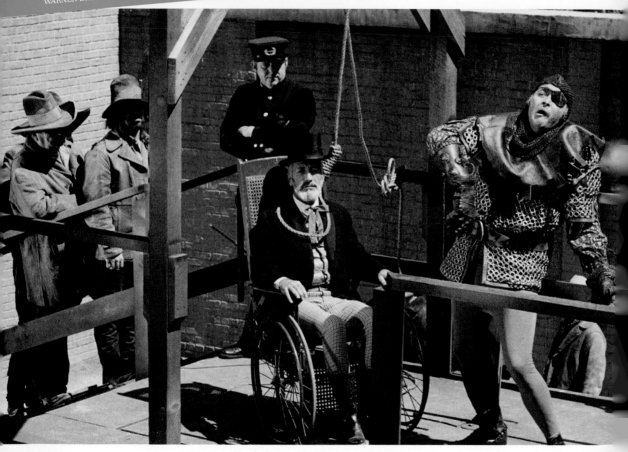

A NIGHTMARE ON ELM STREET 5:
THE DREAM CHILD (1989)

INDIANA JONES AND THE TEMPLE OF DOOM (1984)

LUCASFILM LTD/PARAMOUNT/THE KOBAL COLLECTION

GRIZZLY (1976)
FILM VENTURES INT/THE KOBAL COLLECTION

DANGEROUS LIAISONS (1988)

WARNER BROS/THE KOBAL COLLECTION

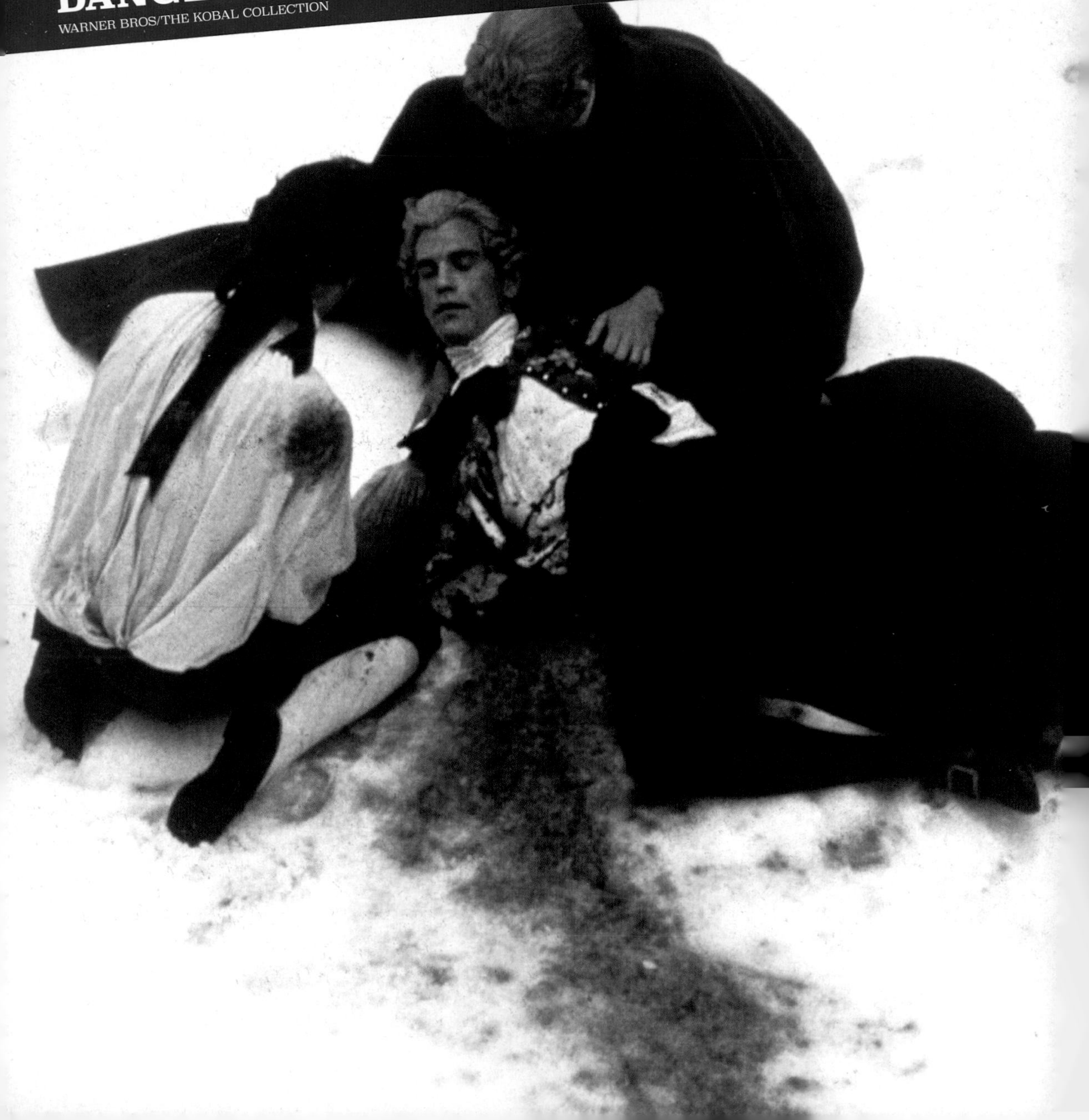

ROCKY IV (1985)
MGM/UA/THE KOBAL COLLECTION

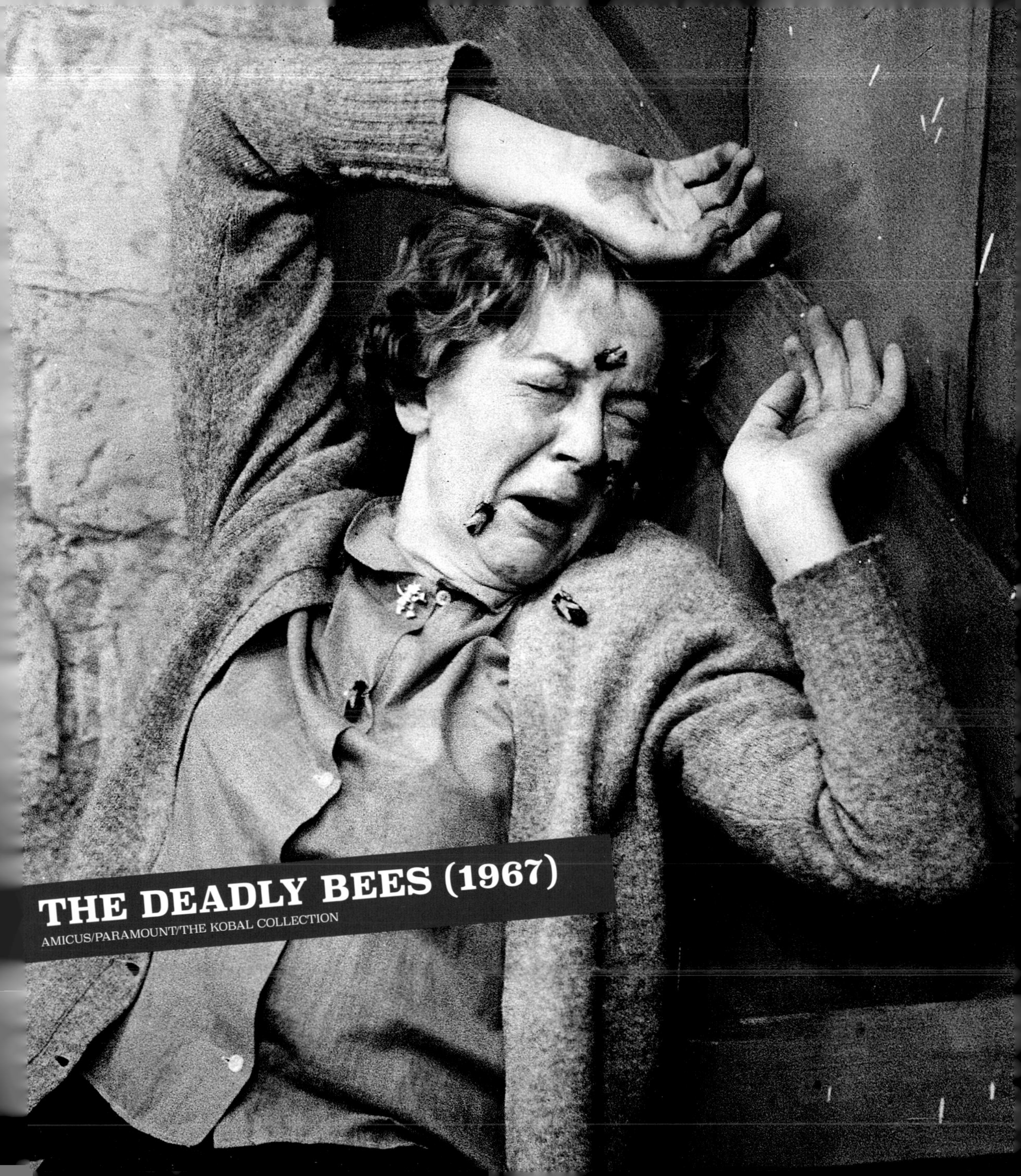

THE DEADLY BEES (1967)

AMICUS/PARAMOUNT/THE KOBAL COLLECTION

THE DAY OF THE TRIFFIDS (1962)

THE MANCHURIAN CANDIDATE (1962)

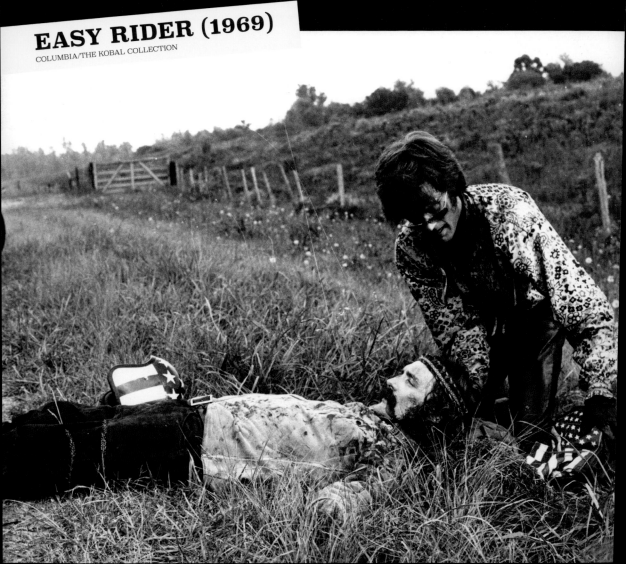

RAMBO (2008)
LIONSGATE/THE KOBAL COLLECTION

GOLDFINGER (1964)
DANJAQ/EON/UA/THE KOBAL COLLECTION

EXCALIBUR (1981)

ORION/WARNER BROS/THE KOBAL COLLECTION

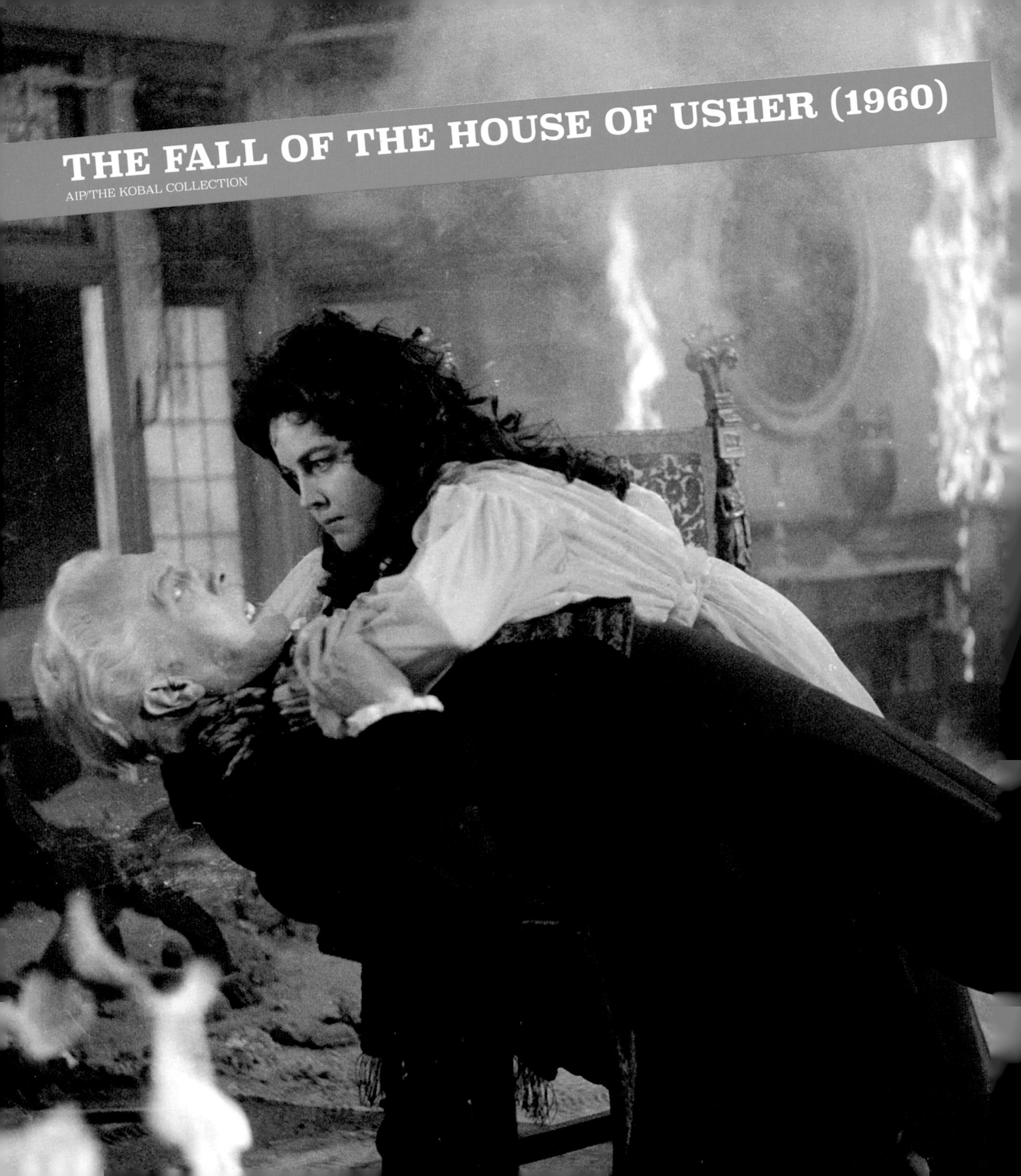

THE FALL OF THE HOUSE OF USHER (1960)

AIP/THE KOBAL COLLECTION

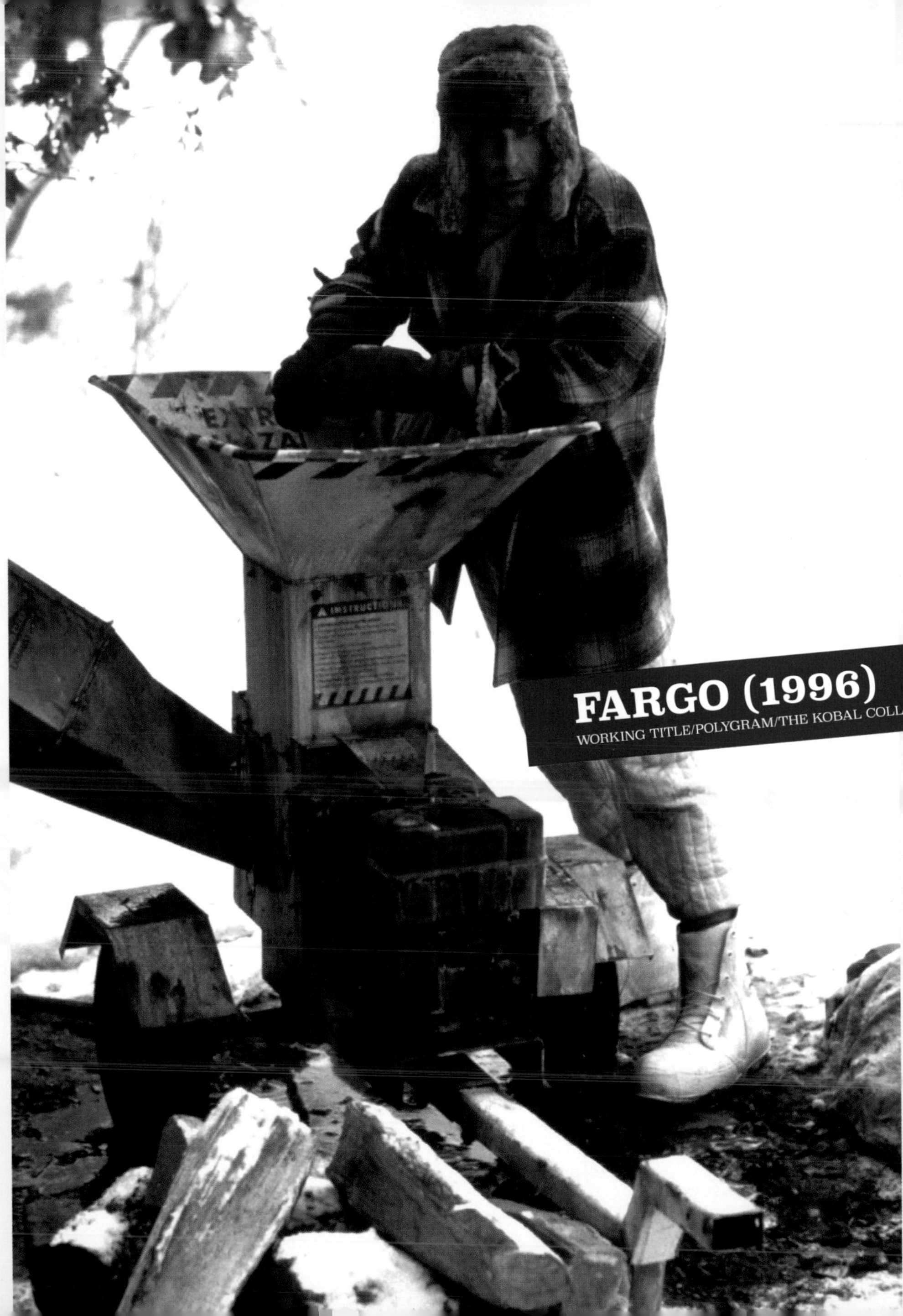

FARGO (1996)
WORKING TITLE/POLYGRAM/THE KOBAL COLLECTION

ANACONDA (1997)

COLUMBIA/THE KOBAL COLLECTION

FROM HELL IT CAME (1957)

SHALLOW GRAVE (1994)

CHANNEL 4 FILMS/GLASGOW FILM FUND/THE KOBAL COLLECTION

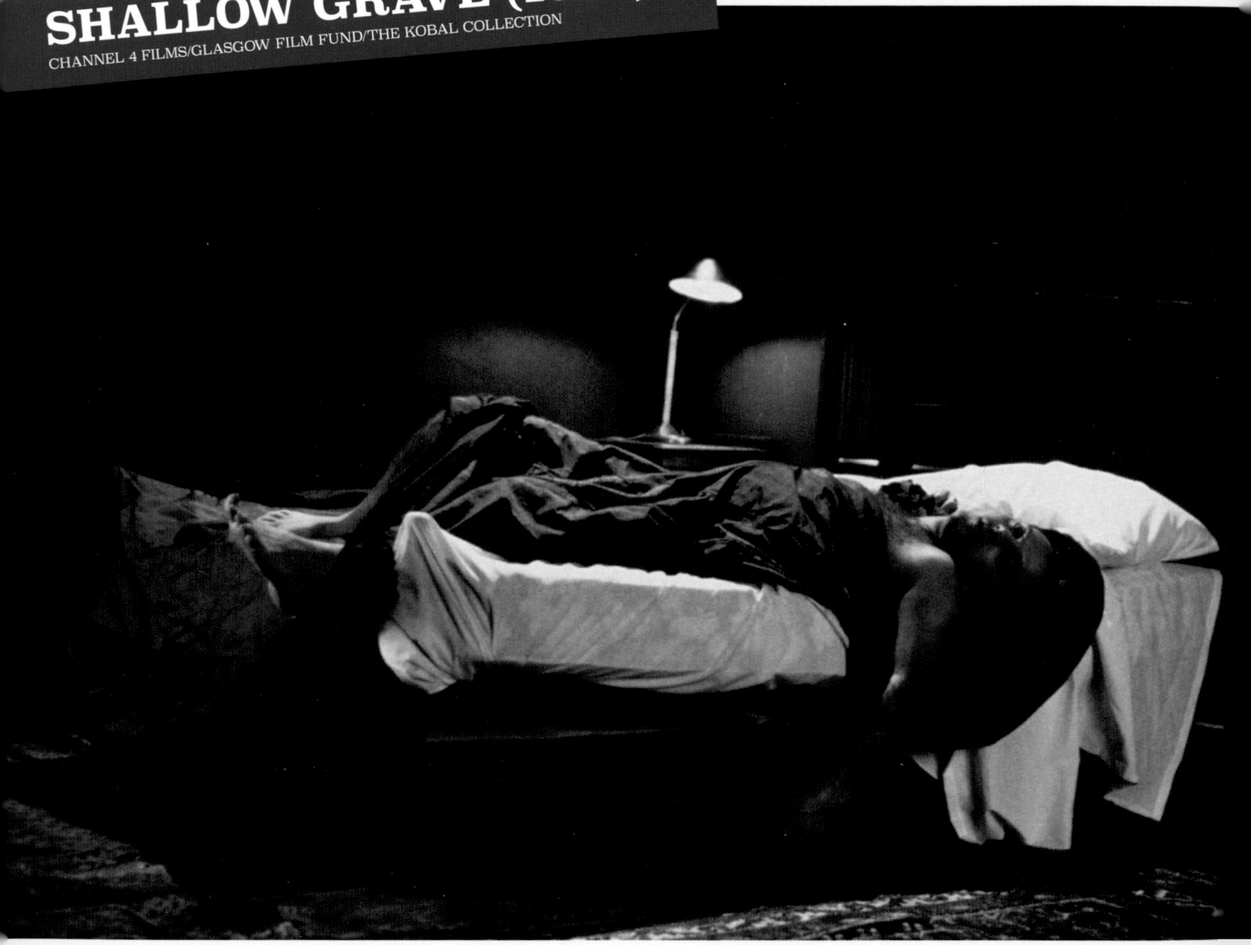

GINGER SNAPS (2000)
LIONS GATE/TMN/TELEFILM CANADA/THE KOBAL COLLECTION

AUSTIN POWERS:
THE SPY WHO SHAGGED ME (1999
NEW LINE/THE KOBAL COLLECTION

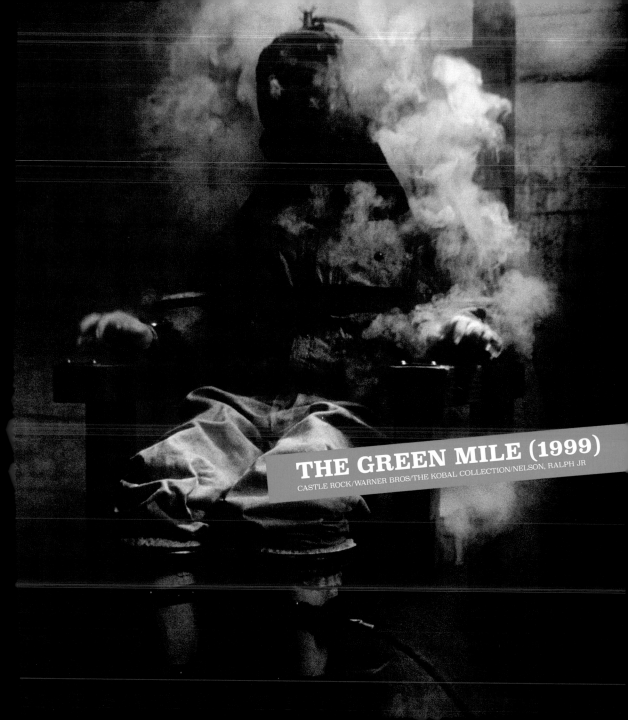

THE GREEN MILE (1999)

PSYCHO (1960)
PARAMOUNT/THE KOBAL COLLECTION

CREEPSHOW (1982)

RAIDERS OF THE LOST ARK (1981)

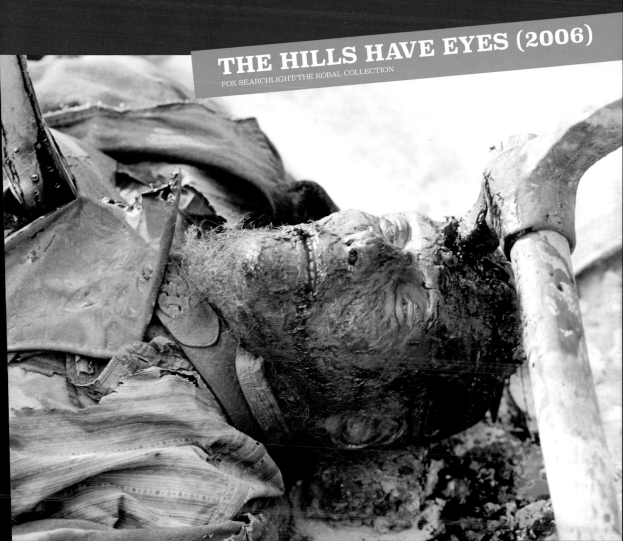

SHARKTOPUS (2010)
SYFY PICTURES ORIGINAL FILM/THE KOBAL COLLECTION

DRACULA HAS RISEN FROM THE GRAVE (1968)

JULIUS CAESAR (1970)

DON'T LOOK NOW (1973)

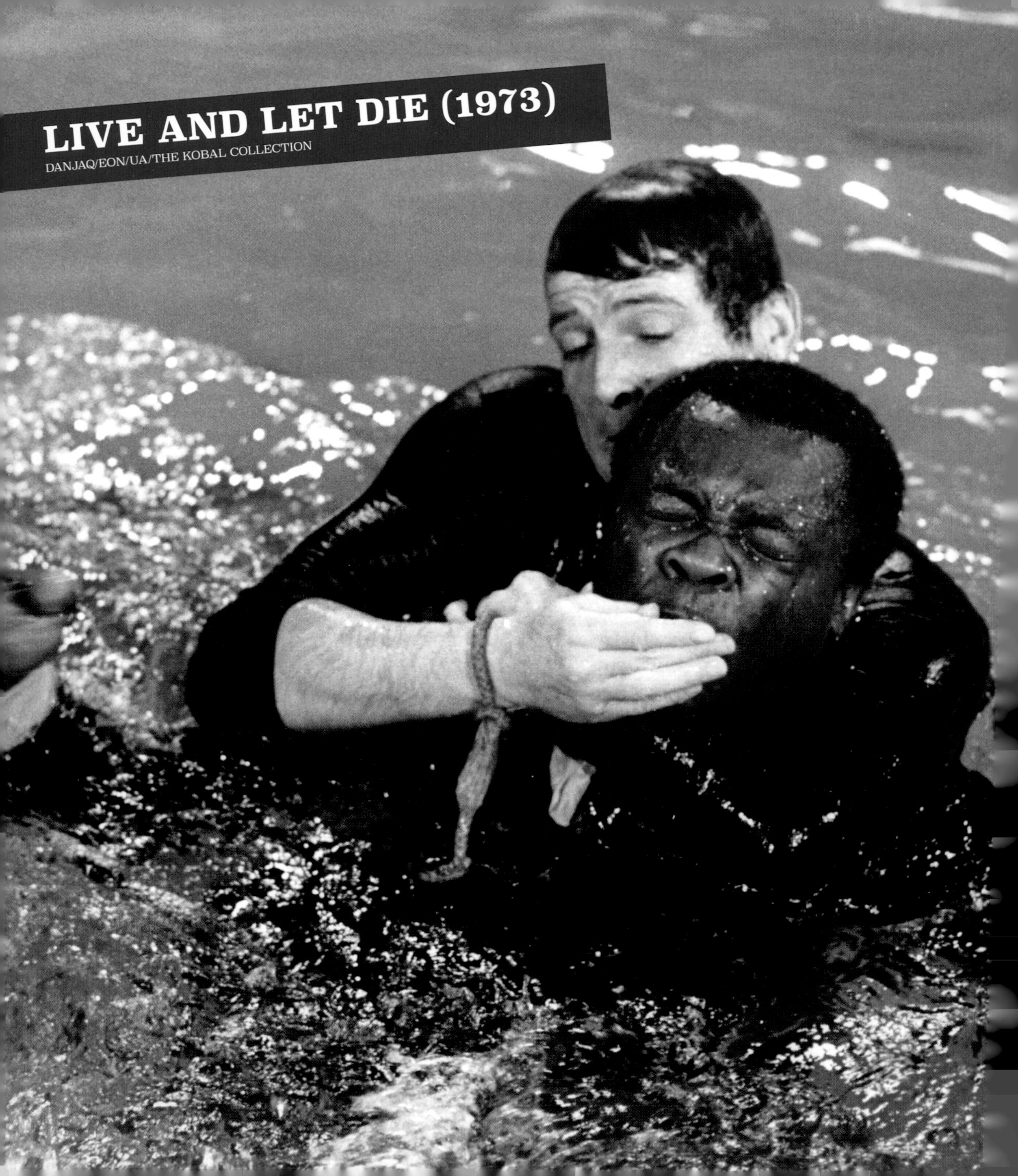

LIVE AND LET DIE (1973)

DANJAQ/EON/UA/THE KOBAL COLLECTION

A MATTER OF LIFE AND DEATH (1946)

MIDNIGHT COWBOY (1969)

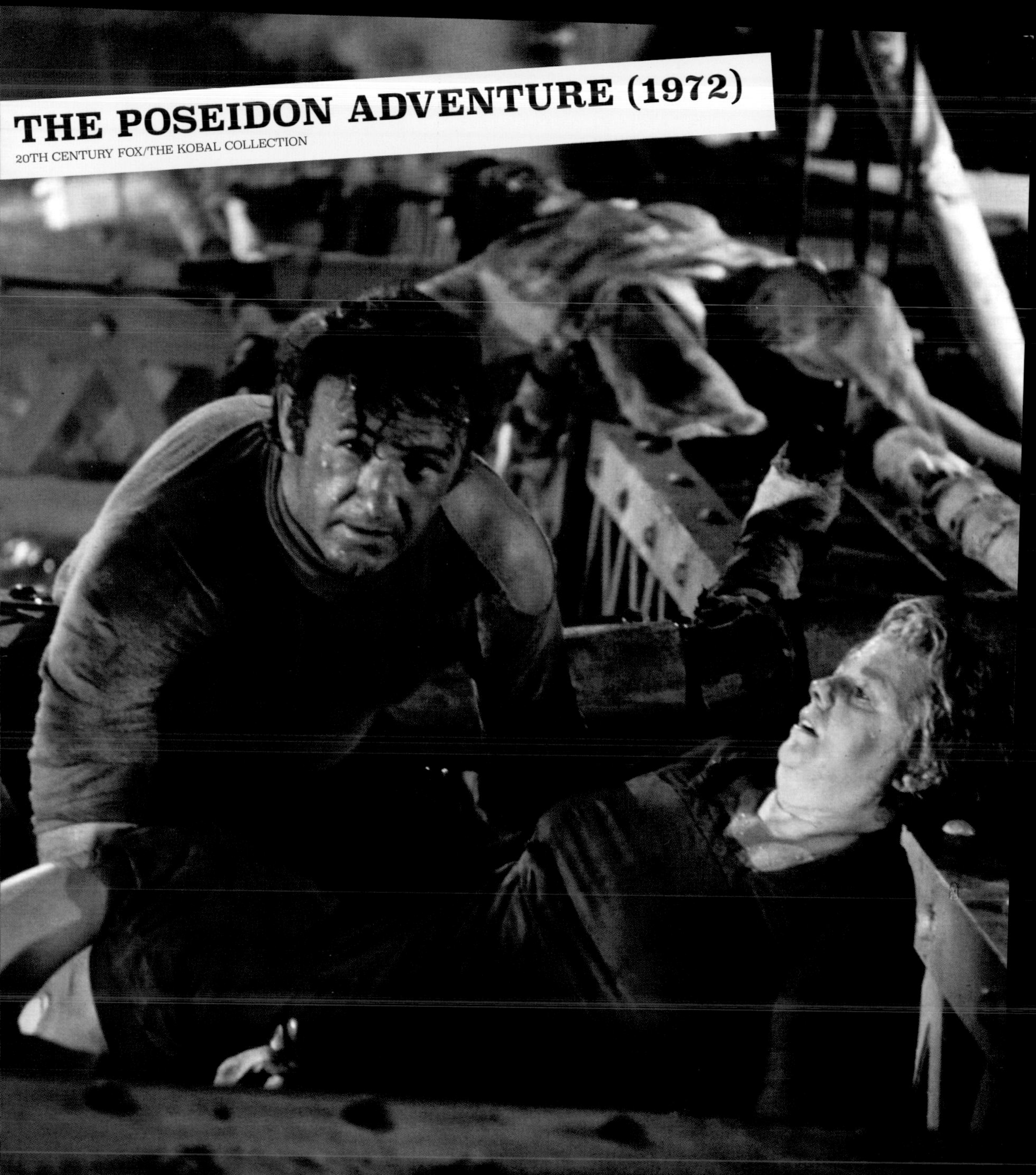

THE POSEIDON ADVENTURE (1972)

20TH CENTURY FOX/THE KOBAL COLLECTION

GREMLINS II: THE NEW BATCH (1990)

THE BEAST OF HOLLOW MOUNTAIN (1956)

PROM NIGHT (1980)
AVCO EMBASSY/THE KOBAL COLLECTION

QUARANTINE (2008)
ANDALE PICTURES/THE KOBAL COLLECTION

DELIVERANCE (1972)

WARNER BROS/THE KOBAL COLLECTION/HAMILTON, JOHN

STAR WARS EPISODE IV:
A NEW HOPE (1977)
LUCASFILM/20TH CENTURY FOX/THE KOBAL COLLECTION

CLEOPATRA (1963)
20TH CENTURY FOX/THE KOBAL COLLECTION

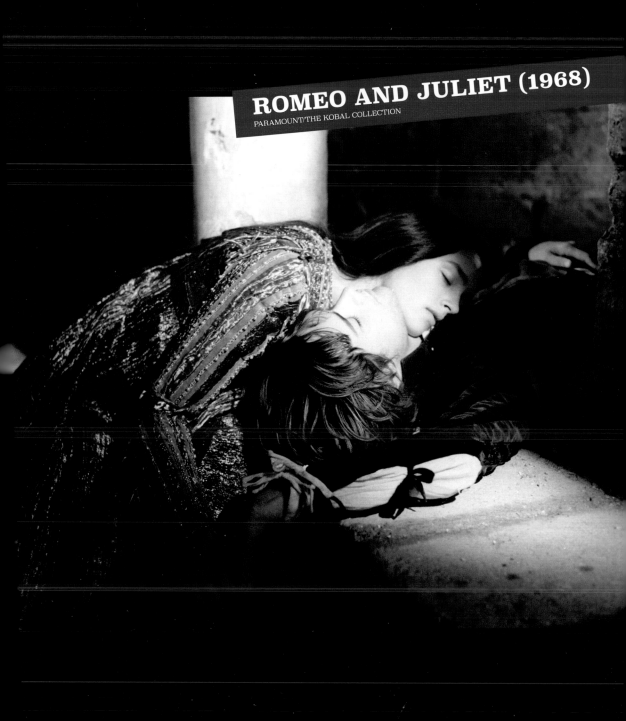

BLACK SHEEP (2006)

LIVESTOCK FILMS/NEW ZEALAND FILM COMMISSION/
THE KOBAL COLLECTION/GEORGE, KEN

THE FROZEN DEAD (1966)

HOT SHOTS! PART DEUX (1993)

20TH CENTURY FOX/THE KOBAL COLLECTION

SPECIES (1995)
MGM/THE KOBAL COLLECTION

STRANGERS ON A TRAIN (1951)

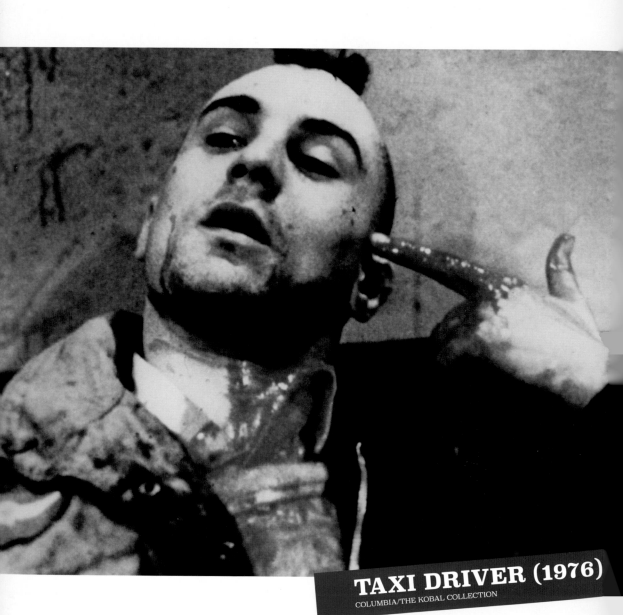

THE VAMPIRE LOVERS (1970)
HAMMER/AIP/THE KOBAL COLLECTION

THE TOWERING INFERNO (1974)

TO KILL A KING (2003)

THE WICKER MAN (1973)

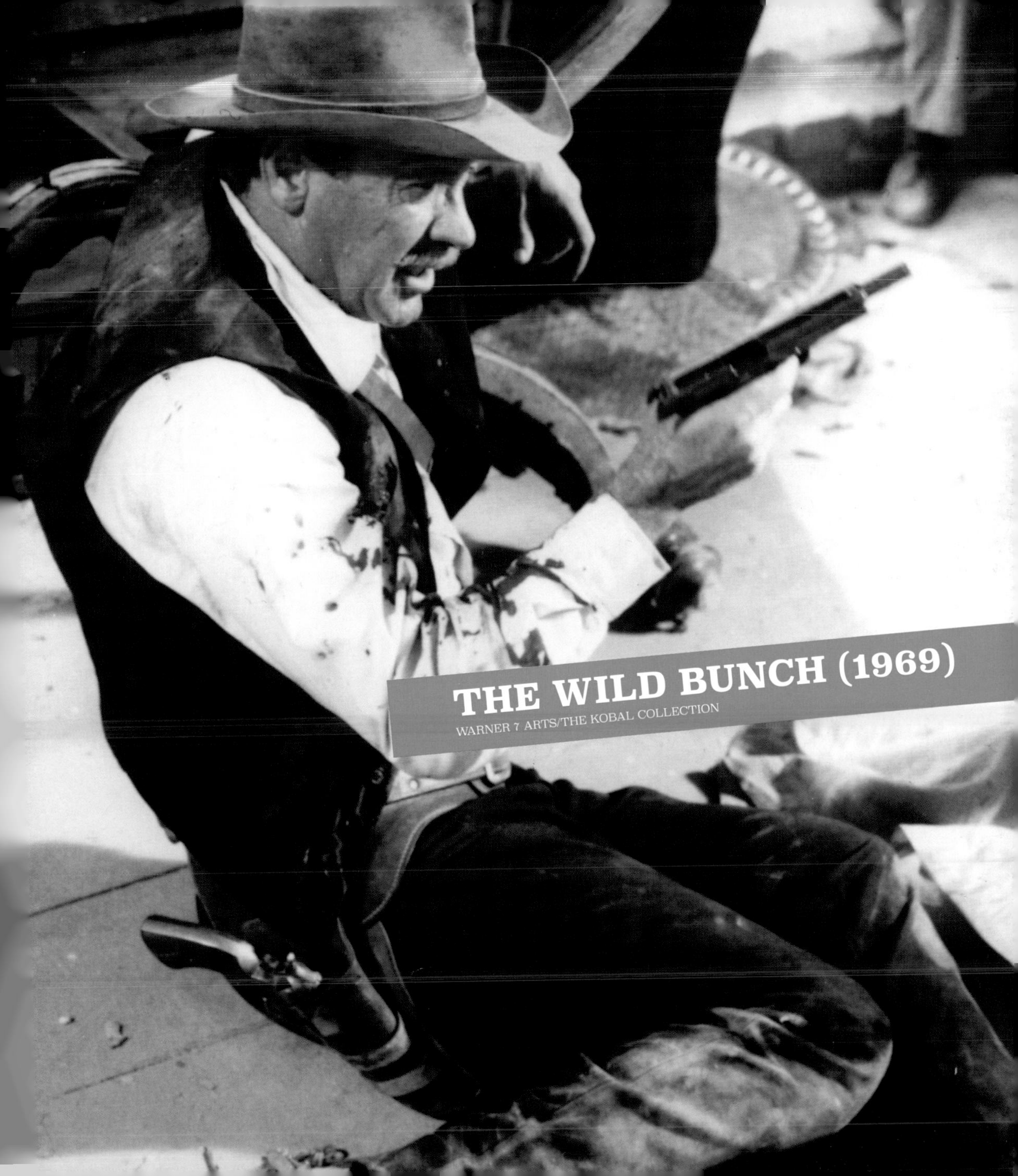

THE WILD BUNCH (1969)

WARNER 7 ARTS/THE KOBAL COLLECTION

THE WIZARD OF OZ (1939)

You might be interested
in these other great books from
Tumbleweed & The History Press

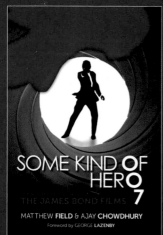
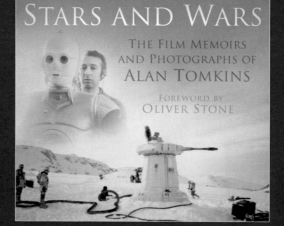
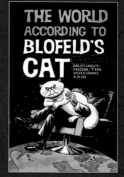